# — LEEDS CASTLE, KENT —

### A ROYAL RESIDENCE (EDWARD I – HENRY VIII)

Stations:- Hollingbourne 1 ½ miles. Maidstone 6 miles.
London within 50 miles.

A HISTORICAL ORIGINAL MEDIEVAL CASTLE SITUATED
IN A MAGNIFICENT PARK, COMMANDING EXTENSIVE
VIEWS, FINE SUITE OF ENTERTAINMENT ROOMS,
20 PRINCIPAL 7 SECONDARY BEDROOMS,
COMPLETE SERVANTS' ACCOMMODATION 7 OFFICES.

TO LET PARTIALLY FURNISHED WITH 3,200 ACRES
FIRST RATE SHOOTING KENT (In a pretty part of the
Country, on the healthy Kentish Ragstone, about 6 miles
south-east of Maidstone and 1 ¼ hours rail from London).

↑ *To Let - Leeds Castle, The Times, March 13, 1925.*

# INTRODUCTION

For centuries Leeds Castle has brought people together for relaxation, reflection, entertainment and hospitality. Set in a landscape designed for aesthetics rather than defence and owned by powerful women, from medieval queens to a wealthy Anglo-American heiress, it has hosted influential events and famous figures. In common with many English castles, Leeds has a complex and fascinating history. Over the years it has been transformed from a medieval royal retreat to an elegant twentieth century country house. Its transformation is a story of rescue, restoration and, above all, passion.

Leeds Castle's foundations date from 1119; however little remains of the original, relatively modest Norman fortification built on a series of small islands in a lake formed from the River Len. Eleanor of Castile (1241-1290), Queen Consort of Edward I, acquired the castle in 1278 and her remodelling of

the castle can still be seen in the gloriette – a D shaped building on its own island and linked to the rest of the castle by its own two-storeyed stone bridge – and courtyard, the only surviving elements of the original medieval castle. Five succeeding medieval queens were associated with Leeds Castle and for the next three hundred years it remained a Royal residence, before passing into private hands in 1552. The fluctuating fortunes of succeeding generations of interlinked families created a cycle of minor repairs, neglect and costly renovation. Sold in 1926 to pay crippling death duties, the castle was bought by an extraordinary woman, one with seemingly unlimited supplies of drive, ambition, and wealth. Under the patronage of the Hon. Olive, Lady Baillie (1899-1974), Leeds Castle was reimagined as a luxurious country house retreat. Managed by the Leeds Castle Foundation since 1974, we welcome all our visitors as esteemed house guests.

*The Mill and Barbican, c.1290s.*

# ESTATE MAP

1. The Castle
2. The Gloriette
3. The Maiden's Tower
4. The Gatehouse
5. The Mill and Barbican
6. The Moat
7. The Culpeper Garden
8. The Lady Baillie Mediterranean Gardens
9. The Great Water
10. The Princess Alexandra Gardens
11. The River Len

2

1

3

6

4

5

7

8

9

10

11

←N

0 —— 100
METRES
(APPROX.)

# — ◇ CONTENTS ◇ —

*Thorpe Hall Drawing Room.*

# THE LEEDS CASTLE
## — STORY —

In 1925, the future of Leeds Castle was uncertain. The golden age of the English country house had come to an end with the onset of World War I, and the death of hundreds of young heirs on the battlefields of France. Post-war taxation and crippling death duties resulted in a rush to sell land and property. Hundreds of country houses were demolished, their interiors sold to architectural salvage firms. Many of England's architectural gems were shipped to America, purchased by public museums or millionaires with a taste for the past. Leeds Castle could have suffered a similar fate, without the timely intervention of a wealthy Anglo-American heiress.

## DESIGNED TO ENTERTAIN AND AMAZE

Unlike the great fortifications of Dover or Rochester, Leeds Castle was constructed on a domestic scale and had been in private hands for generations. Fairfax Wykeham Martin (1887-1952), who inherited the estate on the death of his father in 1924, had never taken up residence. In common with many owners of enormous 'gothic piles', he preferred to live in relative ease and comfort elsewhere. Yet despite decades of neglect, the property retained its romantic 'old world' charm, living up to its epithet as 'the loveliest castle in the world', a term coined by the art historian and politician Sir Martin Conway (1856-1937), who in 1905 rescued nearby Allington Castle from ruin. However, as other well-intentioned owners had discovered to their cost, restoring and maintaining a large historic property required a healthy bank balance, as well as competent architects and visionary interior designers. The redoubtable Wykeham Martin was possessed of a business acumen perhaps lacking in his ancestors. With no inclination to spend his own money, Leeds Castle was initially listed in *The Times* (13 March 1925) as a rental property, to be let by agents Knight, Frank & Rutley as a suitable country house retreat with 'six spacious entertaining rooms, 20 principal bedrooms and plenty of room for servants'. Wykeham Martin added an additional five per cent on the £1000 per annum rent to cover any necessary improvements required. There were, perhaps unsurprisingly, no takers and by the summer he had decided to sell the castle. For a time it seemed that the fabulously wealthy American newspaper tycoon William Randolph Hearst (1863-1951) might buy it, but the lack of even the most basic of amenities proved too much of a challenge, even for someone as rich as Hearst.

But not for a young twenty-seven year old heiress the Hon. Olive Wilson Filmer. In common with many wealthy couples in the early decades of the twentieth century, Olive and her second husband Arthur (1895-1968) had a mind to buy a country house retreat. Close proximity to the capital was a prerequisite, and so they set off from their house in London's fashionable Belgravia to view potential rental properties in Kent. Olive was independently wealthy, with an American mother, the heiress Pauline Payne Whitney (1874-1916), and an English father, the industrialist Almeric Paget (1861-1949). She had received a cosmopolitan upbringing, moving to England with her parents in 1902 and, as a young woman, being educated in France. Her mother furnished the family's London home in what was then called 'the French style'; commissioning walls hung with old gold and grey-blue brocade and rooms furnished with sixteenth-century Italian furniture and treasures from her own father's extensive art collection. Olive's husband Arthur adored antiques and had a particular passion for English furniture, tapestries and textiles. Their union, although short lived, was one of impeccable taste. It was also convenient when it came to buying Leeds Castle. Arthur inherited his maternal uncle's nearby estate of East Sutton Park, with its Elizabethan manor house, which had been remodelled in the eighteenth and nineteenth centuries and Wykeham Martin had made it clear he would only negotiate with those with Kentish connections. Preferring to buy rather than rent, Olive's offer of £180,000 – a sum equivalent to about £12 million at today's values – was accepted and, after a protracted conveyancing process, the sale was completed in 1927. Olive Wilson Filmer was now chatelaine of Leeds Castle.

*Dining Room Tapestry (detail), c.1780.*

13

## THE 'NEW' CASTLE

Having purchased their dream home, the Wilson Filmers were under no illusion as to the extent of the renovations necessary to make Leeds Castle not just habitable but more in keeping with a modern sensibility. When the Wykeham Martin family inherited Leeds in 1821 it was in a parlous state: the mill and barbican were in ruins, and gatehouse was in disrepair, the Tudor Maiden's Tower was in imminent danger of collapse, the main house (embellished in the eighteenth century in a Gothick style) was decaying and the gloriette was more or less a ruin. In 1822, Fiennes Wykeham Martin (1759-1861), Fairfax's grandfather, demolished the main house and replaced it with something which was a late-Georgian version of Tudor, and which was subsequently called the New Castle. He also repaired the gaping hole in the gloriette and cleared and cleaned the moat. But declining family fortunes prevented further modernisation. Consequently, in 1927 little had changed since the nineteenth century: the castle lacked central heating, electric lighting and even the most basic of bathrooms. Indeed, the primitive plumbing was one of the main reasons why William Randolph Hearst withdrew his interest. Undeterred by the formidable task ahead, and with a seemingly limitless project budget of around £100,000 (a not inconsiderable sum in 1927), Olive embarked on a journey to create her personal vision of an imagined medieval castle, albeit one fit for an elegant twentieth century lifestyle.

→ *The gloriette during restoration, c.1920s.*

# FRENCH CONNECTION

Sir Martin Conway took more than twenty-five years to restore the medieval ruin that was Allington Castle, in contrast Olive was a woman not known for her patience. She immediately employed the services of British architect Owen Little (1866-1931) to reorganise the ground floor of the New Castle, beginning with the creation of an inner hall, the construction of a stone staircase and the transformation of the nineteenth century Great Hall into a library. For the upper floors of the New Castle, and the redesign of the gloriette, Olive looked further afield, engaging the French designer-decorator Armand-Albert Rateau (1882-1938). By all accounts, Little and Rateau enjoyed a productive working relationship, even holidaying together at Rateau's home at Bougival on the Seine, a fashionable suburb outside Paris and a source of inspiration for impressionist artists. By 1926, Rateau had established himself as the designer du jour for a wealthy elite who could afford to have homes across the globe. Throughout the 1920s he also worked for the French couturier Jeanne Lanvin, designing the iconic Arpège perfume bottle. He also decorated and arranged the interiors at

Lanvin's legendary Pavillon de l'Elegance at the 1925 Exposition Internationale des Arts Décoratifs et Industriels Modernes in Paris, the exhibition that gave Art Deco its name.

↑ *Armand-Albert Rateau in front of the Gatehouse.*
← *Renovations in the gloriette, 1927.*

# MONEY NO OBJECT

It is likely that Rateau's introduction to the Wilson Filmers was orchestrated by one of their wide circle of influential friends or acquaintances. As Olive spoke impeccable French, communication with her designer held no language barriers and their close working relationship is still in evidence in the castle today. In common with many such restorations of the period, Leeds Castle combines original features, albeit rearranged to suit Olives exacting demands, with new interventions. In creating a glorious French gothic fantasy, Rateau completely gutted the gloriette, creating an entirely new bedroom suite with ensuite dressing room and glamorous marbled bathroom. The 'great hall' was restored to its full size (it had previously been divided into china closet, kitchen and scullery), creating a fabulous room for entertaining. Little also designed a new circular staircase at the north end of the salon, providing a 'secret' means of escape for the lady of the house from the endless round of entertaining. The nineteenth-century chapel was gutted, panelled and converted into a writing room/music room with a new-fangled radiogram that piped music around the castle. A handsome stair tower, made in Rateau's workshop and brought direct from France, was constructed against the south wall of the fountain courtyard. The slightly dishevelled crusader atop the newel post was so authentic it was often mistaken for a genuine antique. No expense was spared; even the servants' quarters were completely modernised, with plumbed hot and cold running water, a rare luxury for many who spent their lives 'below stairs'. Throughout all the renovations, Olive cracked the whip, so much so that only a year after she and Arthur bought the castle, they were able to welcome guests in their new salon.

*Lady Baillie's bedroom, redesigned by Boudin, 1935/6.*

# OAK & STONE

Little and Rateau both had a passion for traditional working methods and simple materials such as oak. Indeed, the refurbishment of the castle became a creative collaboration between European and English craftsmen; Italian and French carvers were employed by Rateau to carve new oak beams for the salon. Jacob Long & Sons of Bath, a firm with experience in country house renovations, realised Owen's designs for the Estate lodges and entrance gates, stables, garages and laundry. They were also contracted to convert the Maiden's Tower from a brewhouse into bachelor apartments. Realising that the destruction of some of

England's finest houses presented him with some great opportunities, Rateau sourced historic interiors from various architectural salvage companies. An Elizabethan chimneypiece was purchased from Woodlands Manor, a medieval manor house in Wiltshire, whilst the antique dealers Acton Surgery supplied the panelling and chimney piece from Thorpe Hall, a seventeenth century house in Peterborough. Some original features from the nineteenth century refurbishment of Leeds were also retained, including carved stone Tudor chimney pieces and fireplaces, original firebacks and a carved oak overmantel.

*French Caen stone fireplace, 16th century.*

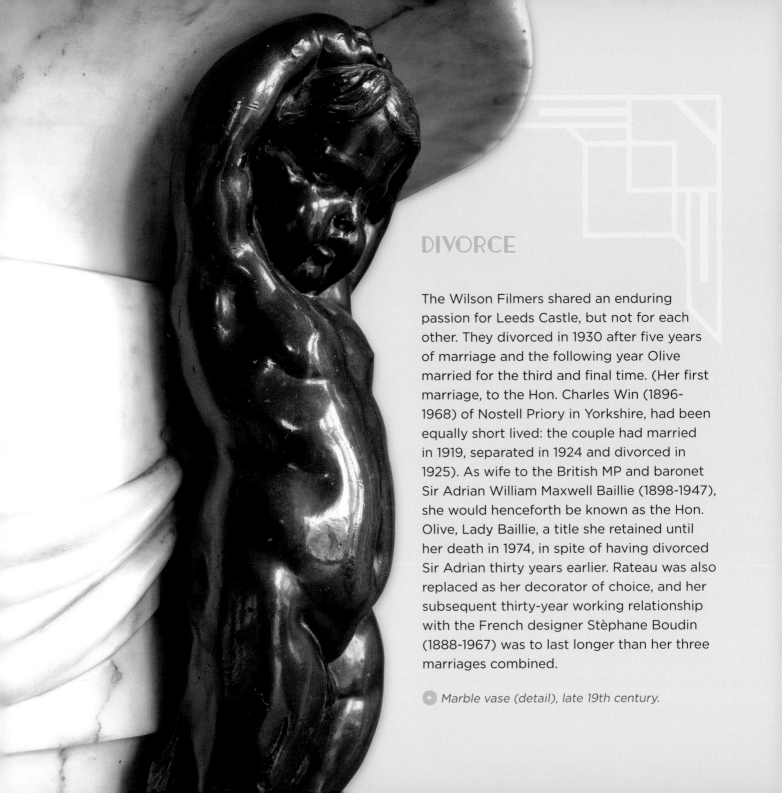

## DIVORCE

The Wilson Filmers shared an enduring passion for Leeds Castle, but not for each other. They divorced in 1930 after five years of marriage and the following year Olive married for the third and final time. (Her first marriage, to the Hon. Charles Win (1896-1968) of Nostell Priory in Yorkshire, had been equally short lived: the couple had married in 1919, separated in 1924 and divorced in 1925). As wife to the British MP and baronet Sir Adrian William Maxwell Baillie (1898-1947), she would henceforth be known as the Hon. Olive, Lady Baillie, a title she retained until her death in 1974, in spite of having divorced Sir Adrian thirty years earlier. Rateau was also replaced as her decorator of choice, and her subsequent thirty-year working relationship with the French designer Stèphane Boudin (1888-1967) was to last longer than her three marriages combined.

← *Marble vase (detail), late 19th century.*

*The Dining Room.*

## BOUDIN

Boudin was president of Maison Jansen, a leading decorating firm in Paris, with clients who included the Duke and Duchess of Windsor (who were also guests of Lady Baillie at Leeds) and, in the 1960s, Jacqueline Kennedy. The glamorous and luxurious interiors that Boudin created in Leeds Castle from 1936 onwards reflect a lifestyle that was played out against the gathering storms in Europe, where guests such as the German ambassador Joachim von Ribbentrop, an inveterate country house guest, could still mingle with British royalty. In addition to designing some of the exquisite interiors of Leeds, and reworking several of Rateau's early designs, Boudin also decorated Harbourside, Lady Baillie's home on Paradise Island in the Bahamas, and her town house in Belgravia.

# KEEP CALM AND CARRY ON

At the outbreak of World War II, Lady Baillie and her daughters Pauline (1920-1984) and Susan (1923-2001) by her first husband, and her son Gawaine (1934-2003) by her third, moved into the gloriette, and the New Castle served as a hospital; many of the ill-fated British Expeditionary Force repatriated after the fall of Dunkirk in 1940 were cared for here, and it was also used for the rehabilitation of severely burned pilots treated by the brilliant plastic surgeon Sir Archibald McIndoe (1900-1960) at East Grinstead Hospital. Weapons research was secretly carried out on the Estate, including the development of emergency flame weapons to counter the feared German invasion.

*Pauline and Susan, c.1930s.*

# INTERNATIONAL WOMAN OF MYSTERY

Life at the castle after the war was more restrained than it had been in the 1930s. The gloriette was shut up and used mostly for storage, the glamorous parties abandoned. Lady Baillie established an annual progress, spending the spring and early summer in England, staying during the week at Lowndes House, her London mansion, and travelling down to Leeds Castle each weekend. Late July, August and early September were spent in the south of France, where she had a villa in Cap-Ferrat, and where she passed her time shopping, drinking and gambling in the casinos of Monte Carlo or entertaining friends like David Niven and Nöel Coward. Then it was back to Lowndes House and Leeds for the autumn, before a three-month stay at Harbourside in the Bahamas. Through it all, Leeds Castle remained her favourite residence.

*Lady Baillie's vanity case.*

ALD 840

# COUNTRY HOUSE
## —◆— WEEKEND —◆—

'The perfect place in which to spend a weekend is undoubtedly Leeds Castle near Maidstone, where the Hon. Mrs Wilson Filmer and her husband have been giving one of their usual house parties.'
**Daily Mail, Tuesday 18 September, 1928.**

*Lady Baillie, Sir Adrian and the Dowager Lady Baillie, c.1930s.*

# 'FASHIONABLE FOOLS'

Leeds Castle is a rare survivor from the heyday of country house living and entertaining. Whereas in the aftermath of World War II, many owners faced increasing pressure to open their doors to a paying public, Leeds Castle remained essentially a private home, whose doors were only opened to an invited social set. Unlike some country house owners who perhaps ventured out of London half a dozen times a year, Lady Baillie travelled home to Leeds Castle every weekend. She filled her home with an eclectic mix of Tudor portraits, tapestries, antique furniture from France and Spain, chinoiserie objects and ceramics. She also collected exotic wildlife, filing the Estate with zebras and llamas, as well as aviaries full of exotic birds. As the daughter of the 1st Baron Queensborough and a New York heiress, Olive was well versed in social etiquette; and the role of generous hostess was written into her DNA. Her salon was always open to a wide range of acquaintances who could be relied upon for good conversation and witty repartee. Her admirers included glamorous film stars like David Niven, James Mason and the unpredictable Errol Flynn, the politicians David Margesson and Geoffrey Lloyd, and, in the words of author and diarist Henry 'Chips' Channon 'fashionable fools'. Olive was well acquainted with the Astors and Vanderbilts (the latter were close friends of her parents) and the former Mrs J J Astor, one-time chatelaine of Sutton Place, Guildford, was a frequent guest at Leeds in her new role as Lady Ribbledale. Margaret, Duchess of Argyll, whose colourful private life attracted so much media attention in the 1960s, also frequented Leeds.

David Niven with his
wife Hjördis Genberg

Douglas Fairbanks Jnr.
with Academy Award
and Loretta Young

Douglas Fairbanks
and Mary Pickford

Noel Coward

Errol Flynn

James Mason

31

# LEISURE & LUXURY

*'Mrs Wilson Filmer has a distinct flair for interior decoration, and has successfully raided all Europe for tapestries, brocades, rare carpets, and furniture.'*

**Daily Sketch**, 1929.

Lady Baillie's 'court' also included a large coterie of gay men. Before the Sexual Offences Act (1967), homosexual acts between men over the age of twenty-one were illegal; and Leeds Castle provided a safe haven for Olive's many gay friends, away from the prying eyes of the gossip columns and media. With her indomitable drive and inherent good taste, house parties at Leeds were always well planned and provisioned, although she would often desert her guests and retire to a corner of the salon to watch her favourite films.

Indeed, Olive adored the movies so much she created her own cinema in the Maiden's Tower. Even the austerity of the war years failed to make its mark: in August 1943 Chips Channon wrote in his diary 'we sunbathed, overate, drank champagne, gossiped all day'. For those less inclined to loll in a deckchair, more strenuous activities could involve a couple of games of tennis, or use of the indoor squash court, a swim in the pool, complete with wave machine or a stroll in the park, carefully avoiding the zebras and llamas roaming the grounds.

*The Pulchinello's Kitchen by Giovanni Battista Tiepolo, 18th century (detail).*

# SOCIETY HOSTESS

Olive was a seasoned gambler, spending the late summer months in a villa in Cap-Ferrat and the casinos of Monte Carlo. At Leeds, guests were expected to join her in the Games Room for canasta and bridge and, certainly after their first stay, would be resigned to losing heavily. Whilst she could be extremely generous in terms of hospitality, she had her particular quirks. If her guests made excessive use of the telephone provided in each bedroom, an itemised bill would be discreetly placed there before their departure. Even the austerity of the war years failed to make much of a mark on the social life of guests. Whilst Lady Baillie and her family moved into the gloriette, handing over the New Castle to the military for use as a hospital, weekends continued in much the same way. Geoffrey Lloyd, the government minister responsible for the secret weapon research carried out in the grounds of Leeds Castle at this time, remained a close friend of Lady Baillie, eventually becoming the first Chairman of the Leeds Castle Foundation.

*'The tables are Monte are always surrounded. So far Lady Bailey (sic), who has forsaken the beauties of Leeds Castle for the distractions of Monte, is the big noise in the gambling way. One of the very few in fact to play really high and give the onlookers something to see and talk about.'*

**The Tatler, 1933**

 *Yellow Drawing Room.*

LADY BAILLIE
BATH Rᴹ

SIR ADRIAN
BED Rᴹ

BATH Rᴹ      DRESSING Rᴹ      YELLOW

SECRETARY
OFFICE      BED Rᴹ

WALNUT
BED Rᴹ      BATH Rᴹ

NURSERIES
BATH Rᴹ

NIGHT

HENRY VIII
DRESSING Rᴹ   BATH Rᴹ

BED Rᴹ

# BELOW STAIRS

A vast retinue of staff was required to support this lifestyle. During the 1920s and 1930s, increased taxation and crippling death duties had a profound impact on the running of country house estates, which was an expensive undertaking. Some owners economised by reducing their staff, dispensing with senior manservants in favour of parlour-maids, who were paid less. Lady Baillie, however, retained her hierarchy of staff working at Leeds Castle, with each employee having a carefully defined role. Apart from the office staff, such as the land agent and secretaries, the indoor staff normally included a house steward, butler, under-butler and three footmen, plus a nursery footman, hall boy and odd-job man. Her French chef had five kitchen maids and the housekeeper was in charge of eight housemaids. Six or seven gardeners worked in the grounds, under the head gardener, and there were various other groundsmen, chauffeurs, laundry staff, grooms and gamekeepers. Staff were not restricted to working in the Castle: Borrett the butler, accompanied her on her annual progress to the South of France and the Bahamas.

'Beyond the gate-house is a wide courtyard, the Inner Bailey, at the far end of which stands the castle and the main entrance. Men and maid-servants were gathered in the hall, evidently enjoying the novelty of showing people round. In charge of a tall and aloof manservant, I made a progress through a series of living rooms, where long windows provided a glimpse of the waters of the moat below.'

**I Saw Two Englands, H.V. Morton describing a visit to Leeds Castle, 1939.**

← *Bell box, circa 1930s.*

# WOMEN OF POWER
# SOURCES OF WEALTH

Leeds Castle has a long history of female ownership and patronage. The medieval queens who owned the castle were raised and educated in cosmopolitan European courts and were trained to manage complex households, act as royal advisors and intercede with the monarch on behalf of their subjects. They left their homes accompanied by an entourage of women, some high born to act as friends and advisors, others more lowly to perform tasks assigned to servants. Marriage provided courts not only with the prospect of fulfilling dynastic ambitions, but also opportunities for cultural connections – the brides brought with them not only dowries, but also their own language, literature, styles of dress and art. Different in appearance, speech and manners and accompanied by their foreign retinue, their very presence elicited awe, suspicion, and jealousy. Fundamental to any royal marriage was the prospect of a significant dowry, both land and money supported England's kings in their ambitions to regain rights to overseas dominions and avoid costly wars. Eleanor of Castile (1241-1290), Queen Consort to Edward I (1239-1307) established the precedent for queens to own property in their own right. Medieval queens were financially vulnerable, a king was expected to make financial provision for his wife, consisting of income and estates, in order that she could support herself and her household in a manner befitting her rank and station. However, should their husband die, a queen became dependent on her dower, which could be seized by future kings, or the largesse of their families. Eleanor was raised in a culture where women were expected to acquire and manage an extensive property portfolio. This, and the revenues gained from her estates, provided financial security, not only for herself but also for the queens who followed her.

39

# ELEANOR (1241-1290)

Eleanor has been accused, both in her own time and in later accounts, of avarice in her drive to acquire an endowment for herself via the acquisition of estates. She acquired Leeds Castle in 1278 from William de Leyburn (his father was a key ally of Edward's grandfather in the Barons' War (1264-1267)), who himself acquired the Estate from Roger de Crevecoeur, a member of Eleanor's household. This exchange of properties, mostly driven by the need to relieve family debts, was not unusual. As well as Leeds Castle, Eleanor also acquired further properties in Kent, as well as Essex, Suffolk and Cambridge.

Whilst Edward I concentrated on building imposing fortresses to suppress the rebellious princes in Wales, Eleanor played an important part in transforming Leeds Castle from a standard Norman motte and bailey stronghold into a glorious medieval fantasy, inspired by her Spanish upbringing. The gloriette, although destroyed and rebuilt over the centuries, is a lasting legacy of her impact on the architecture of the castle, influenced by her childhood exposure to the art and architecture of Islam. The foundations of the courtyard in the castle are also tangible reminders of Eleanor's lasting influence as a royal arbiter of taste and references the Spanish/Islamic taste for water gardens. She also introduced an aviary at Leeds, possibly populated with swans, Sicilian parrots and nightingales. Medieval courts were always on progress between royal residences, however records state that the couple spent a total of 51 nights at the castle, including Edward's 40th birthday. Leeds Castle was in easy reach of Dover and travel to the continent and Canterbury, where offerings could be made at the altar of the martyr St Thomas Becket (c.1118-1170). Eleanor had exquisite taste and her aesthetic, one of lavish decoration and domestic luxury, reflected royal wealth and power. She invested heavily in creating the perfect retreat for herself and her husband, filling the royal apartments in the gloriette with luxurious Spanish woven carpets and tapestries, jewelled plate and glass imported from France and Venice, and created a sumptuous wardrobe from the finest and most expensive fabrics. She also installed 'the King's Bath house' widely believed to be the first of its kind in England. Documentary evidence states that it was paved with 'one hundred Reigate stones'.

*Foundations of the courtyard date from 1290s.*

Eleanor's personal and intimate objects were lost or destroyed over time; however evidence of Edward I's 'bath house' exists within the water gate, underneath the walls of the bailey and adjacent to the Maidens' Tower.

An effective manager as well as a formidable queen, Eleanor's luxurious home also operated as an administrative hub for her portfolio of Kentish properties. However, Eleanor's acquisitions were not wholly supported by the country. The Chronicle of Walter of Guisborough (1272-1312) recounts a highly critical commentary made by some young squires 'The King would like to get our gold/The queen, our manors fair to hold'. She was also castigated by Archbishop Peckham of Canterbury, who rebuked her for profiting from usury – the practice of acquiring lands indebted to Jewish moneylenders. Whilst this may have proved unpalatable to Peckham, Eleanor was simply following normal practice at the Castilian court; her family entrusted all their financial administration to members of the Jewish faith.

*Effigy of Eleanor of Castile.*

43

# MARGARET
## (1279-1318)

Eleanor's taste and wealth created a fabulous love nest nestled in the valley of the River Len. She also established the precedent for English queens to own property in their own right. On the death of his beloved wife, Edward created lasting monuments, the Eleanor Crosses, to mark the progress of her coffin from York to London. When Edward was 60, he married his second wife Marguerite of France (1279-1318), the first French queen of England. She brought with her a dowry of £15,000 (equivalent to approximately £10.6M), as well her youth and vivacious nature. In return she received all land and property formerly belonging to Eleanor, including Leeds Castle. Margaret was fond of music, games and hunting and Leeds provided the perfect backdrop to such courtly pursuits. However, there is little documentation or physical evidence of Margaret's stays at the castle beyond the fact that she spent her honeymoon there with Edward.

→ *Stone carving of Margaret of France.*

# ANNE
## (1366–1394)

Subsequent royal brides also enjoyed the informality of Leeds Castle: Anne of Bohemia (1366-1394), Richard II's (1367-1400) beloved wife, spent the Christmas before her wedding in the castle, and she and Richard returned regularly, using it as a retreat from the stifling formalities of court. Her tragic death in 1394 did not deter Richard from visiting the castle several times, although such visits were mainly on state business rather than purely pleasure.

*Queen Anne of Bohemia and King Richard II, manuscript, 1382.*

*Isabella and her son Edward III, detail from illuminated treastise by Walter de Milemete.*

# ISABELLA (1295-1358)

On Margaret's death in 1318, Leeds Castle, should have passed directly to Isabella of France (1295-1358), Queen Consort to Margaret's step-son Edward II (1284-1327). He married Isabella when she was 12 years old, a year after becoming king. Cultured and well educated, Isabella was shocked by the lack of elegance at the English court, and by allegations of her husband's alleged homosexuality. In a surprising breach of protocol, Edward granted Leeds Castle to his male favourite, Bartholomew de Badlesmere, Lord Steward of the royal household. This was only one of a series of slights against his queen, however despite Edward's ill treatment of her, Isabella played a significant role in one of the most dramatic events in the history of the castle.

Edward was a weak and feeble ruler, whose policies and relationship with another favourite, Hugh Despenser, actively alienated the barons. Despite his early affiliation to the crown, Badlesmere changed his allegiance to that of the rebel lords. In 1321, despite the tensions within their marriage, Isabella collaborated with Edward in an act designed to accelerate the tensions between crown and rebels. Isabella arrived at Leeds Castle with a small retinue of followers, allegedly seeking rest whilst on pilgrimage to Canterbury. Isabella had every right to expect a warm welcome – the castle was hers by royal prerogative. However, in the absence of Bartholomew and on the direct orders of her husband, Lady Badlesmere refused entry. In what can only be described as a face-off between two strong-willed women, Isabella attempted to force entry to the castle. Lady Badlesmere responded in kind, commanding her archers to attack the interlopers. Six of Isabella's tiny army were killed, and the King swiftly responded by accusing Badlesmere of treason. The castle was placed under heavy siege for two weeks; Lady Badlesmere's attempts to hold out were thwarted by the inability of her husband to muster support for his cause from the rebel lords. She eventually capitulated, and Isabella and Edward's revenge was brutal. Lady Badlesmere and her children were banished to the Tower of London, and twelve of her men were hanged. Badlesmere was also hanged and decapitated in Canterbury – his spiked head a gory reminder of the perils of displeasing his King and Queen. On the death of her husband, Isabella eventually took possession of Leeds Castle in her own right; she also inherited a crystal and jade chess set that had once belonged to Eleanor.

# JOAN (1368-1437)

Medieval society did not readily accept women in positions of wealth and power. Joan of Navarre (1368-1437) was financially independent and married her second husband Henry IV (1367-1413), in 1403. Neither had a dynastic reason to marry and it appears their union was, to all intents and purposes, a love match. Henry followed the tradition of his forebears and granted Leeds Castle to his wife soon after their marriage. With the King's permission, she in turn granted Leeds to the Archbishop of Canterbury, Thomas Arundel (1363-1414) in 1412. After Henry's death in 1413, Joan initially enjoyed good relations with her stepson, Henry V (1386-1422) but her position as queen dowager became increasingly vulnerable. Henry was faced with providing a dower for both his stepmother and his prospective wife, Catherine de Valois (1401-1437). In 1419, in a desperate attempt to take control of Joan's finances, Henry accused her of plotting his death by 'the most horrible manner that one could devise'. Witchcraft was not made a capital offence in England until 1563, however it could have serious ramifications, including a death sentence. Joan was imprisoned without trial first at Leeds Castle and then in solitary confinement in Pevensey Castle. She returned to Leeds in March 1422 in Sir John Pelham's (died 1429) charge, where she was allowed to live in relative comfort, as evidenced by her wardrobe book, now in the Leeds Castle collection. Henry had a change of heart before he died in 1422, possibly realising that the charges were at best spurious, and restored Joan's dower to her. However, the stigma of witchcraft remained throughout Joan's life, highlighting the plight of many women who found themselves at the mercy of their male relatives.

→ *Effigies of Joan and Henry IV.*

R̄ · DE · FRANCE ·                    h̄ · LE · CINQVIESHE ·

Le premier chapitre de
mon stre comment le

erte marie de mon seigneur
sainct Denis patron de sran

# CATHERINE (1401-1437)

Henry V married the glamorous and popular Catherine de Valois (1401-1437), youngest daughter of Charles VI of France in 1420 in a union that was seen to unite both countries. The marriage was short lived, Henry's unexpected death left Catherine a young widow and mother of the future King Henry VI. As a queen dowager, with no prospective daughter in law, Catherine received a large inheritance, including Leeds Castle, and was able to maintain her own sophisticated household. Her subsequent affairs scandalised the court but her eventual marriage to Owen Tudor (1400-1461) led to the creation of the Tudor dynasty. Her grandson by her second marriage was Henry Tudor (1457-1509), who in 1485 became Henry VII, father of Henry VIII (1491-1547). Catherine was the last medieval queen to own Leeds Castle.

*The marriage of Catherine de Valois & Henry V.*

# KATHERINE (1485-1536)

Leeds Castle underwent significant changes in the 16th century, under the auspices of Henry VIII. As the younger brother, Henry did not expect to accede to the Crown, however the death of Arthur, Prince of Wales (1486-1502) catapulted Henry into the limelight. On the death of Henry VII in 1509, Henry was 18 and as a young, inexperienced king, had not yet discovered the insatiable need to assert his power via the building and acquisition of magnificent large palaces such as Nonsuch and Hampton Court. Between 1517-1523, Henry commissioned major alterations to Leeds Castle after his marriage to his Spanish born wife, Katherine of Aragon (1485-1536). Highly educated and multi-lingual, Katherine had married Arthur in 1502 and was widowed within a year. She continued as a member of the royal court for seven years, finally marrying Henry after the death of his father. The intimate nature and distance from London enabled the young married couple, who had endured a long courtship, to escape the prying eyes of the court at Greenwich and Whitehall.

Leeds Castle was never a permanent residence for Katherine and Henry. For many years it was thought that Katherine and Henry, along with a court numbering more than 5,000, stayed overnight in May 1520 at Leeds Castle on their way to the Field of the Cloth of Gold. The diplomatic event was staged to strengthen the bonds of unity between the ancient rivals, however it was also an opportunity for both kings to indulge in extraordinary displays of wealth and magnificence. The evidence to support the supposition that Leeds Castle hosted the Royal Court centres on the additional funds Castle Constable Sir Henry Guildford (1489-1532) received in May 1520, which also coincided with the period of major renovations of the castle. Based on the most recent research, it is unlikely the event took place; there are only four documented accounts of Henry visiting Leeds Castle between 1422 and 1544, resting en route to Dover, Canterbury and Rochester.

*Katherine of Aragon, c.1520.*

Katherine would have been familiar with the Islamic influenced architecture of the gloriette and central courtyard, a style prevalent in Spain from the 12th to the 15th centuries. From the inventory taken in 1532, on the death of Sir Henry Guildford who supervised the work, the principal royal apartments were still in the medieval gloriette and an upper floor had been added. Material evidence in the form of stone motifs on fireplaces, testify to the promise of their early union. Henry relied on Katherine's good counsel – she was the first female ambassador in European history – and embellished the castle with symbols of their love. A ragstone fireplace survives in Lady Baillie's Private Writing Room; the spandrel on the left contains the arms of the House of Lancaster, from which the Tudors are descended, and the Tudor dragon with a serpent added to its tail. The spandrel on the right contains the castle of Castile and pomegranates of Aragon. The pomegranate is a Christian symbol of fertility and eternal life. Deeply religious, Katherine trusted in God to bless her union with Henry. Whilst she had six pregnancies, two sons did not survive infancy and only one girl survived to adulthood. Whilst at court, Henry was responsible for all Katherine's housekeeping expenses, including food for her household. He also provided for her wardrobe, as well as clothing and shoes for her servants. Exiled from court once

Henry decided to marry Anne Boleyn (1500-1536) in 1533, and with her marriage annulled, Katherine was denied a queen's dowry and had to meet all her own expenses. She died all but penniless in 1536, in Kimbolton Castle in Cambridgeshire, deprived of her court, friends and even her beloved daughter, Mary (1516-1558) who would eventually become Queen of England (1553-58).

# PRIVATE OWNERSHIP

With its royal connections and its beautiful location, not to mention its proximity to London, Leeds Castle was an attractive proposition for any individual looking for a physical embodiment of their status. Its combination of Norman and Medieval antecedents, together with Henry VIII's remodelling, offered an enduring sense of a cultured life, one that embraced all the benefits of country house living. The reality of owning such a property was less romantic. In 1552, after nearly 300 years in royal ownership, Edward VI (1537-53), Henry's only legitimate son by his third wife, Jane Seymour (1508-37), transferred title to a royal favourite, Sir Anthony St. Leger (1496-1559) of Ulcombe, near Leeds, for a yearly rental of £10.00. Sir Anthony's grandfather had been Constable of the castle. As Lord Deputy of Ireland, he had been instrumental in subjugating the uprising in Ireland, creating Henry VIII King of Ireland.

# SMYTHE FAMILY (1618-1632)

After Sir Anthony's death in 1558/9, the Leeds Castle Estate passed into the hands of his younger son, Sir Warham St. Leger (1526-1559). In 1617, Sir Warham invested heavily in Sir Walter Raleigh's (c.1554-1618) ambitious expedition to Guiana in search of the legendary El Dorado (1595), fitting out and commanding one of the explorer's ships. The 'City of Gold' expedition turned into a complete fiasco, and the fleet returned, disillusioned and with nothing to show for their endeavours. The adventure financially ruined Sir Warham, who in 1618 was forced to sell the castle to a wealthy relation, Sir Richard Smythe (1565-1628), although there is a suggestion that he may have acquired the castle before 1599. Smythe had both business and political connections. His father,

Thomas Smythe (1522-1591), was a member of Parliament and collector of customs duties for Elizabeth I (1533-1603) and purchased Westhanger Castle, Kent in 1575. Richard's brother, Sir Thomas Smythe (1558-1625), was the first governor of the East India Company and treasurer of the Virginia Company. Sir Richard had a talent for marrying wealthy widows: Elizabeth Scott (m.1589), Jane White (m.1598) and Margaret Langdon (m.1610). Smythe owned property in Colman Street, London and Salmeson Grange, Margate, which once belonged to St Augustine's, Canterbury.

The 17th century was the start of a great period of rebuilding in England and the introduction of a more classical approach to country house design. Shortly after coming into possession of Leeds Castle, Smythe instigated dramatic changes: he demolished all the surviving medieval buildings at the northern end of the main island and replaced them with a Jacobean style manor house, symbolically embellished with the Smythe coat of arms. The foundations were discovered during repair works to the present castle in 1993, and it is clear that this was a substantial mansion. Sir Richard died in 1628, leaving the castle to his son, Sir John Smythe (1591-1692), he also left a charitable bequest of £6 to the poor 'of the parish of Bromefield, Kent'. Sir John survived his father by only four years; he died in 1632

without an heir and the castle passed to his two married sisters, Lady Elizabeth Thornhill (1595-1626) and Mrs Mary Barrow (1601-1666). The same year they sold the castle to Sir Thomas Culpeper (1578-1661), who gifted it to his son, Sir Cheney Culpeper (1601-1663), a supporter of Elizabeth Stuart (1596-1662), daughter of James I and the exiled Queen of Bohemia. Paradoxically, Sir Cheney was on the side of the Parliamentarians during the English Civil War (1642-51), which probably helped save the castle from destruction. Dover Castle remained in the hands of the Parliamentarians despite coming under siege by the East Kent Royalists.

↑ *The damaged gloriette, 1822.*

# CULPEPER FAMILY (1632-1719)

Like previous private owners, Sir Cheney's finances were in a precarious state, and in March 1651 he secured a loan against the castle. He continued to reside at Leeds until 1663, when he died embittered and in debt. His creditors sold the castle to a kinsman, Thomas, 2nd Lord Culpeper (1635-1689). Raised in a Royalist household in the Netherlands, Thomas returned to England following the restoration of Charles II. His father, John, had accompanied the Stuart royal family into exile at the start of the Civil War, and was rewarded for his loyalty to the Crown with the grant of more than five million acres of land in Virginia, which would be cultivated as tobacco plantations. In 1659 Thomas married Margaretta van Hesse (1635-1710), a wealthy Dutch heiress and together they had one daughter named Catherine (b.1667). In 1664, he was appointed Governor of the Isle of Wight, where he lived openly with his mistress, Susanna Willis (circa 1610-1670), with whom he had two daughters. He leased the castle to the government as a place of detention for Dutch and French prisoners of war, captured during the Second Anglo-Dutch War (1665-1667). The diarist John Evelyn (1620-1706) had the task of marching the 500 prisoners, a 'sick flock' from Maidstone to the castle. Lodged in the gloriette, the unruly mob on one occasion set fire to their accommodation. Evelyn fails to mention the event in his diary, but does record that he 'flowed the drie moate and made a new draw bridge, brought also Spring Water into the Court of the Castle to an old fountaine, & tooke order for the repaires', which may be a reference to the damage. The gloriette would not be substantially repaired until the next major rebuilding of the castle site in 1822. After the repatriation of the prisoners, Margaretta lived at the castle, where she died in 1710. In 1677, Thomas was appointed Governor of Virginia and went on to increase his land holdings in America, some 300,000 acres in the Shenandoah Valley, which eventually fell, as Leeds Castle did, to his only legitimate daughter, Catherine.

*Catherine Culpeper, c.1690.*

# FAIRFAX FAMILY (1719-1800)

Catherine married Thomas, 5th Lord Fairfax of Cameron (1657-1710), a MP and Scottish peer, in 1685. As was the custom, upon marriage Catherine's substantial fortune, and Leeds Castle, passed into the hands of her husband. The Fairfaxes would go on to play a major role in America, significantly increasing their landholdings and owning much of the northern neck of Virginia over their years of ownership. However, Thomas did not manage his money wisely, he embarked on a risky business venture to search for treasure from shipwrecks in the West Indies, which turned out to be financially disastrous. When Thomas died in 1710, he left his family with numerous debts, forcing them to sell ancestral estates in Yorkshire, and Leeds Castle fell into disrepair. It was inherited by his son, Thomas 6th Lord Fairfax (1693-1781), an altogether more astute individual. He maintained an expensive lifestyle financed by the income generated through the Belvoir plantation and estate, located on the Potomac River in Fairfax County. Thomas first visited Virginia between 1735 and 1737, eventually relocating to America permanently in 1747. At his death in 1781, he owned a large

number of enslaved people, and quantities of gold, silver, plate, china, furniture and books.

On Thomas' departure to America in 1745, Leeds Castle passed to his brother Robert Fairfax (1707-93), who held it for 46 years. In that time, he undertook a large-scale programme of costly repairs and improvements, facilitated by the wealth of his two wives: Martha Collins (d.1743), a banking heiress and Dorothy Best (d.1750). The exterior of the Jacobean mansion was clad in imitation of the then fashionable 'Strawberry Hill' Gothic Revival style. Before the visit by King George III (1738-1820) and Queen Charlotte (1744-1818) following a review of the army at Coxheath in 1778, he spent large sums refurbishing the drawing rooms for his royal guests. The Virginia lands were confiscated during the American Revolutionary War (1775-1793), however in 1792 Robert received £13,758 by Act of Parliament for the relief of American Loyalists. Unfortunately, Robert failed to fund the much-needed structural improvements to the gloriette and by the end of the 18th century it was deteriorating badly.

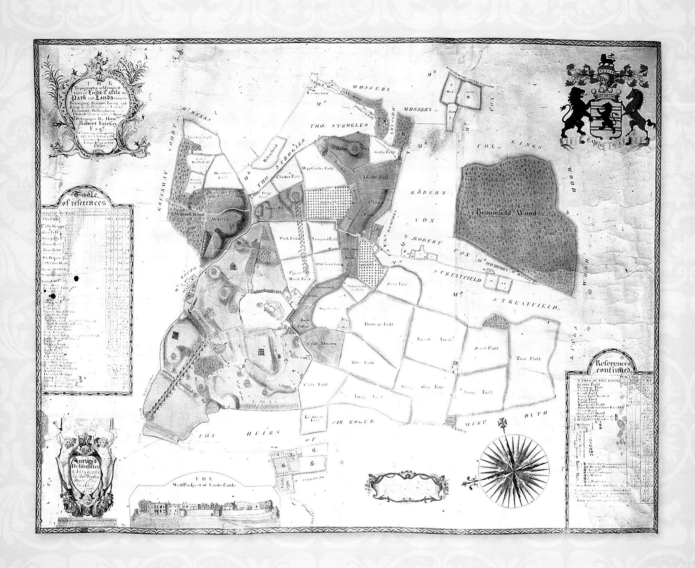

*Hogben map of the Estate, 1748.*

## MARTIN FAMILY (1793-1821)

Despite marrying three times, Robert, 7th Lord Fairfax died without a direct heir. The Leeds Castle Estate passed to his nephew the Reverend Denny Martin (1725-1800), Catherine Culpeper's grandson. Denny never married and on his death in 1800, his brother General Philip Martin (1733-1821) inherited Leeds Castle, where he lived with his three unmarried sisters, Frances (b.1727-1813), Sibylla (1729-1816) and Anna Susanna (1736-1817). This was not an act of charity on his behalf, as they were each charged £100 per annum in board. Philip Martin had a successful military career, participated in the Siege of Gibraltar in 1782 and was praised by the famed British Army Officer General James Wolfe (1727-1759). He also benefitted financially from Virginia, buying additional land and enslaved people to work it. In 1806 the American properties were sold. The sale ended one hundred and fifty-seven years of direct influence over large swathes of Virginia by the Culpeper and Fairfax families.

# WYKEHAM MARTIN FAMILY (1800-1926)

On his death in 1821, and with no direct heir, Philip Martin left his entire estate, including Leeds Castle, to Fiennes Wykeham (1769-1840) with the request 'that he assume the name and arms of Martin', which he duly did. Martin also left £100,000 'to be invested in the purchase of Estates to be added to Leeds Castle, and £30,000 to be expended in repairing and improving this beautiful residence'. Interestingly an executor of Martin's was the Reverend St John Filmer of East Sutton, Kent, a relative of Arthur Wilson Filmer, Olive Baillie's second husband.

Fiennes Wykeham Martin had ambitious plans for Leeds Castle, employing a team of designers and architects to remodel the Gothic manor house into a 19th century mock Tudor country home. The gaping hole that had disfigured the gloriette since the 1660s was repaired and the internal walls rebuilt in stone. However, as previous owners discovered, owning and maintaining a castle was an expensive undertaking and Fiennes rapidly incurred large debts. Unable to recover financially and afraid of being sent to a debtor's gaol, he sold the contents of the castle to pay his creditors. When he died in 1840, he was living in sparsely furnished rooms, without the barest of necessities. Fiennes was succeeded by his eldest son Charles (1801-1870) who like many others before him, made an advantageous marriage, which was by all accounts also a love match. His first wife Lady Jemima Mann (1806-1836) was the daughter of an Earl and bought a substantial dowry to the union and he was able to rebuild the family fortune. His second marriage, to Matilda Trollope (1805-1871) was 'sound and sensible'. After Charles' death, the castle passed through the male line until 1925, when his great grandson, Fairfax Wykeham Martin (1887-1952) sold it to Olive and Arthur Wilson Filmer (1895-1968). Together they embarked on a major renovation project which would transform Leeds Castle into a luxurious country house retreat for their family and friends.

→ *Charles Wykeham Martin, 1851.*

# FILMER FAMILY (1926–1974)

↑ *Wedding photograph,
Olive and Adrian Baillie, 1931.*

Mrs Arthur Wilson Filmer was born Olive Cecilia Paget (1899-1974). Her mother, Pauline (1874-1916) was a member of the wealthy American Whitney dynasty. Her father, Almeric Paget (1861-1949), 1st Baron Queenborough, was a Conservative politician and a descendent of the Marquess of Anglesey. When Pauline Paget died at the relatively young age of 41, she left each of her two teenage daughters two million dollars. Prior to Pauline's death, Olive and her sister Dorothy (1905-1960), each inherited two million dollars from their uncle Oliver Hazard Payne (1839-1917), a founder of the Standard Oil Company. Olive's first husband was the Hon. Charles Winn (1896-1968), the second son of Lord St Oswald, whose family home was at Nostell Priory in Yorkshire. They had two daughters, Pauline (1920-1984) and Susan (1923-2001), and rented a variety of houses in the UK and abroad. They divorced in 1925, and in the same year she married Arthur. Despite their mutual love for Leeds Castle, their marriage was relatively short, they divorced in 1931. Olive's third marriage, to the wealthy Sir Adrian Baillie (1898-1947) produced one son, Gawaine (1934-2003) and ended in 1944.

# LEEDS CASTLE CHARITABLE FOUNDATION (1974-PRESENT)

Independently wealthy, well-educated and with impeccable taste, Olive could afford a permanent residence in one of the most affluent parts of London, as well as holiday homes in Saint-Jean-Cap Ferrat, France and Nassu in the Bahamas. When Olive died in 1974, she ended centuries of private ownership. Shortly before her death, she established the Leeds Castle Foundation, to preserve the castle, its collections and interiors, and its estate for the benefit of the public.

← *Chinoiserie phoenix, 18th century.*
→ *Lady Baillie and her daughters, Pauline and Susan.*

## ACKNOWLEDGEMENTS

Designed by Jamieson Eley.
Written by Sue Prichard.
Project managed by Daniel French.
Researched by Catherine Pell.
Photography by Matthew Walker Photography,
Chris Lacey Photography, Paul Dixon Photography
and Sarah Medway Photography,
with the exception of:
© Alamy (pages 42, 43, 44, 45, 49, 53)
© The Governing Body of Christ Church, Oxford (page 46)
© British Library Board. All Rights Reserved /
    Bridgeman Images (page 50).

Contains Ordnance Survey data © Crown copyright and
database right (2023).

## JARROLD
publishing

Published by Jarrold Publishing.
www.jarrold-publishing.co.uk